# To Whom It May Concern

෴

Poems By
Alan Herman

**1JSP**

1 Jersey Street Press   New York, NY 10012

Copyright © 2010 by Alan Herman
All rights reserved

Printed and bound in the USA

First Printing

Library of Congress Cataloging-in-Publication-Data

Herman, Alan 1944-
   To Whom It May Concern: poems / by Alan Herman
   ISBN: 978-0578-05030-0
   I. Title
Library of Congress Control Number: 2010902109

The Author wishes to acknowledge with gratitude for the following:

The Associated Press, for an excerpt from an article entitled, "Frankie Thomas' obituary" (found on page 32 of this text) Used with permission of The Associated Press Copyright© 2009. All rights reserved.

and with great appreciation for their generous gifts of time assisting in the production of this book: Ivan and Marilynn Karp for their careful reading and encouragement; Alex Herman for her eagle editorial eye; the many trainers at the SoHo Apple Store for their patient technical help; and to all those who lent their hand in many, many ways.

Cover Design and Photograph: Alan Herman (photo a detail from an existing print)
Photograph of Author: Drew Herman
Text set in Perpetua

# 1JSP
1 Jersey Street Press • New York, NY 10012

Printed in the United States by Morris Publishing®
3212 East Highway 30
Kearney, NE 68847
1-800-650-7888

For my beautiful daughters, Alex and Drew—by far the greatest joys of my life— and to all who have provided me even the smallest bits of wisdom along the way; to each of them, I will remain eternally grateful.

*Glory be to God for dappled things*—

Gerard Manley Hopkins

∽

"*If I could think that I had sent a spark to those who come after, I should be ready to say goodbye.*"

Oliver Wendell Holmes Jr.

## TABLE OF CONTENTS

| | |
|---|---|
| JOURNAL ENTRY: THIS MORNING | 3 |
| TO WHOM IT MAY CONCERN | 4 |
| THE FALL | 5 |
| NEEDLES ARIZONA: JULY 1948 | 6 |
| WARD AND ME | 7 |
| PANORAMA: ANNUAL PICNIC, PINECREST GARDENS; SUNDAY AUGUST SEVENTEENTH, NINETEEN FORTY-SEVEN | 8 |
| THAT NIGHT | 12 |
| THE LITTLE GIRLS: THE EMPTY NEST | 14 |
| MUTTON | 15 |
| DREAMS | 17 |
| IN THE SUMMER OF 1949 | 18 |
| WAITING OUT THE RAIN | 21 |
| VESPER | 22 |
| SUNSHINE SEEMS THE CLOSEST THING I HAVE EVER KNOWN TO GOD | 24 |
| WOMAN AT THE FRONT DESK OF THE CANDLE-LITE MOTEL | 25 |
| THE NIGHT BEFORE, THE WEATHER RADIO FORECAST RAIN | 27 |
| ON THAT TUESDAY MORNING | 28 |
| SOAP | 29 |
| NOW, AND WITH THE SUMMER ALMOST GONE | 30 |
| ON APRIL TWENTY-NINTH | 32 |
| THERE WAS SOMETHING IRREVOCABLE | 33 |
| EVEN NOW (THE RING) | 34 |

| | |
|---|---|
| ROADS | 35 |
| LAR BARGSTED | 36 |
| THE OTHER NIGHT | 37 |
| A ROMANCE (working title) | 38 |
| I REMEMBER MY MOTHER AT NINETY-THREE OFTEN SAYING IN THOSE FINAL MONTHS BEFORE SHE DIED THAT MAYBE SOMETIMES A PERSON JUST LIVES TOO LONG: CANTATA AT AGE SIXTY; APRIL 2005 | 39 |
| AT THE ICE CREAM PARLOUR | 42 |
| CROSSING THE SUSQUEHANNA | 43 |
| IN MEMORIAM | 45 |
| WOODPECKERS | 46 |
| CAPS | 47 |
| DEAR P | 48 |
| HEADING WEST IN THE ODDLY MILD JANUARY | 49 |
| A POEM ON MY MOTHER'S DYING | 51 |
| TOMATOES: A PARABLE | 52 |
| THE GOOD NEWS IS | 53 |
| JOURNAL ENTRY: SWEEPING THE PORCH IN EARLY APRIL | 55 |
| CLOWNS AND GORILLAS | 56 |
| IN MY DREAM THIS MORNING | 58 |
| ONE AFTERNOON WHILE VISITING IN A SMALL PAINTED ROOM FILLED WITH FADED LIGHT | 59 |
| QUALIFIERS | 61 |
| PAINTING THE HOUSE | 62 |
| WRITING IN WATER | 64 |
| TO MY MOTHER | 65 |
| REFLECTION, AUGUST 1st 2008: ON NASA'S ANNOUNCEMENT OF WATER ON MARS AND THEREFORE POSSIBILITY OF LIFE | 66 |

| | |
|---|---|
| IT WAS EIGHTEEN DEGREES HERE THIS MORNING | 67 |
| GLASSES | 68 |
| ALGEBRA | 69 |
| AT JOE THE BARBER'S | 70 |
| TWO DAYS LATER: AFTER THE FIGHT WITH THE RABBID RACCOON | 71 |
| BRENDA | 72 |
| AFTER | 73 |
| THOUGHTS ON THE FURTHER WISDOM OF POSTPONING JOY, AND HOW AT 63 IT MIGHT NOW BE TIME TO CASH IN MORE | 74 |
| RESONANCE ON THE FIRST DAY OF SPRING: 2006 | 77 |
| SHE WASN'T THERE AGAIN THAT MORNING | 79 |
| FALL COLOR | 80 |
| AFTER A SECOND DATE WITH A WOMAN WITH WHOM I KNEW THINGS WOULD LIKELY GO NOWHERE | 81 |
| BEYOND MIDDLE AGE | 83 |
| I SEE YOU STILL | 84 |
| DEADHEADING THE COSMOS | 86 |
| EPIPHANY: WITH A SHELL-CUT TOE | 87 |
| ON HAVING RETURNED TO THE CITY LAST NIGHT WITH 16-24 INCHES OF SNOW FORECAST UPSTATE STILL DRAWN TO THE ONE WHO IS UNAVAILABLE | 88 |
| JUST A NOTE FROM TODAY | 89 |
| AN AUTUMN REQUIEM | 90 |
| JOURNAL ENTRY: AFTER A LIGHT SEPTEMBER RAIN | 91 |

# To Whom It May Concern

⁖

Poems By
Alan Herman

JOURNAL ENTRY: THIS MORNING

Sitting alone in the early
light—with the sounds of a kettle,
and now and then a quavered song
of a lingering bird, who soon too will leave—

I think of you: still in your rumpled bed,
in a house I have never seen, a hundred miles away in the Berkshires:
how the rain, you said, always makes you feel at home;
and of all the impossibilities; as I wait for you to maybe call.

*Roses are red, violets are blue.*
*Roses are red, violets are blue..*

## TO WHOM IT MAY CONCERN

How it happened is not what matters; the tangle—
the dissonant nest woven from the hurtful brambles—
and shadows of a half remembered song sung once,
that comes, achingly like rusted glass from very far away,.

What matters is: once delusions are lost, everything changes;
eyes see clearly, no longer able turn away in time.
At the beginning—lost— I left baskets by doors where you no longer were:
the streets were empty; there was nothing to breath,

What matters is: at the beginning I was too sick to stand.
Nights of the dark forest closed around me,
and snared me hopelessly in roots and the dangling tangled vines,
as the hidden moon danced laughing behind the clouds.

What matters is: in time I began to learn the way through the black-lit rain;
that sometimes, barefoot along the paths of seashell shards,
new songs appeared, or hands, or smiles—or berry patches beside the way—
and that in time too, the night stars stopped their endless taunting.

What matters is: that there was always someone, without knowing or asking,
who would hold back a curtain, and help to let me pass.
What matters is: some days the sun would warm a spot by the windowsill,
and there I could press my nose to the glass, and smell the other side.

## THE FALL

Those afternoons at the start of the fall that October after school,
I spent alone in my room there on Twelfth Street
as the last brightness of the days slid past
the slatted wooden blinds, and the long darkening began.

Those afternoons when I was nine, in 1954,
I would thumb those magazines that came each week—
past the uniformed soldiers, and the purposeful men in dark wool suits,
standing so self assured, that certainly I too would have to become in time—

and I would linger long, then secretly, at the lurid illustrations
of tight sweatered blonds, featured in the 'Saturday Evening Post',
who, with their gold-hoop earrings, and thrust upturned breasts,
were all but impossible not to stare at, in what already, seemed shameful ways.

And then there were the ads that came in 'The Ladies Home Journal':
the pairs of stockinged legs with dark welt seams that that rode,
so fearlessly tracing the nylon's smooth,
up and down the sway of those long arcing curves;

women who stood half naked in satin slips,
and floral lace-stitched brassieres, so shamelessly
on those shiny pages—that both transfixed, and made me feel
uneasy— beckoning in their glossy black and white.

How I longed for those dark haired gypsy ladies with a single shoulder bared;
their ribboned hair thrown back in ecstasy, and olive bosom heaved.
My fingers marked the pages to return to, until they would all run out,
or I became too fearful, that somehow they might know.

NEEDLES ARIZONA: JULY 1948

In the early morning diner near a railroad siding, the waitress in the dust filtered light already raises her arm to mop her brow; a fan slowly moves from side to side. Through the momentary hollow of her cuffed uniform sleeve, beyond the slight damp of worn discolored lace near the underarm, the frayed edge of a strap has been marked with a small two-part stain. One stain is somewhat larger than the other; both just below the round adjustment clasp, where it seems, over time, a small chip has been lost from metal's protective coating. Beneath the strap, a tensed swell of smooth flesh pulses. And there is a young boy passing on a cross-country train: he is traveling with his parents to San Francisco; his eyes press beyond the glass. The stains are rust. The strap chafes the woman in the summer heat, at the white softness that still he wants so much to touch.

## WARD AND ME

Across the road that summer when I was four,
    there were boarding stables, and a towhead boy named Ward
I idolized—seven maybe; so able it seemed—and feared might see me as just a kid.

Often in the late afternoons we would walk down their long driveway
    to visit the horses—whose names once I mostly knew—
and we'd bring with us sugar cubes from a diner for the giant Palomino.

She frightened me, that enormous mare—her giant teeth mainly—
    as reluctantly I would hold my hand out, to let her take the gift,
and her rough tongue scraped across my trembling up-faced palm.

Those afternoons outside the barns by the split rail fence enclosure,
    Ward would stand at a certain distance, and call me Captain Seaweed;
and I never understood if he was really teasing, or trying to be my friend.

PANORAMA: ANNUAL PICNIC, PINECREST GARDENS;
SUNDAY AUGUST SEVENTEENTH, NINETEEN FORTY-SEVEN

It appears to be around four-thirty that they took the picture:
the lean man at the back holds the club's banner-staff solemnly —
as he always did no doubt—its satin waves glisten brightly in the late afternoon.

Seated upfront, the club president smiles— coy as a southern sheriff;
head akimbo, fingers clasped around his well sated girth;

a straw hat balances on one knee—and there are small children
sitting on the ground—frozen in time— squinting their eyes against the sun,
restless, impatient to return to play again in the fountain pool.

By count, two-hundred and forty six had come that year
for the annual picnic, each year that third Sunday in August, after church.
And mostly they arrived by streetcar, families and loners,

the young and the old; the sad jokester who always clowned,
and mid-frame among the crowd, the cross-eyed woman who looks away.

A few came with their dusty green DeSotos, or an older two-door Plymouth
with the smell of once spilled milk that never went away;
a dark blue Chevrolet overheats in traffic each year on the road back to town.

Still devoutly each year by one, they all arrived to those public gardens,
and sat on blankets brought from home with baskets lunches
wrapped with gingham, and some with thermos jugs of lemonade.

Each year they passed those foods of all description and shared on paper plates
that late summer day; and pies came after, with high golden crusts

made in their white cupboard kitchens—
of sifted flour with lard or Crisco, rolled out on wooden boards—
and later came watermelon, kept cool in the shade of a wide spreading elm.

A few men, all of whom were badly sunburned by late afternoon,
had brought along some beer, and one a silver hip-flask;
a woman, who also had made chicken as well, cried briefly

that her potato salad did not turn out the way it looked in the magazine;
and that year a man who lived in a rooming house alone,

arrived early, and stood hours at the cast-iron grill
roasting hot dogs he had ordered weeks before from Neblowski's,
the Polish butcher near his work on the other side of town.

After lunch, there were those that would try to play a game of ball,
and others who just sat and talked, told stories, or courted sweethearts
hand in hand; young men in ironed shirts, some still in service uniform,

and the girls with broad-collared floral dresses—hemmed-up the night before;
late in rooms beneath a bare fluorescent fixture—

were careful to adjust their skirts just so.
The day was clear, the and times felt hopeful then,
two years after the end of the war.

And maybe a group of men—who got together only this one time each year—
told how Carl Furillo, had shagged a long laced fly,
the day before, with Ralph Branca on the mound against the Phillies,

down at Shribe Park, before it was Connie Mack;
and how Furillo one-hopped the ball from the far right field corner

to Gil Hodges covering the plate, to nail the lead runner mid-slide,
and retire the side at the bottom of the eighth of a three-three tie, on the radio,
and then how Snider came up, and the Duke had hit one into the stands.

⁂

Some older women— some alone, and some sitting silently with friends,
as others spoke in worried tones of the latest turn in the radio drama
"Young Doctor Malone" that they listened to each day devoutly—

had mostly taken off their polished white summer shoes, so they might feel
once more the grass that afternoon, as it played gently between their toes.

It was that year too, perhaps, that a well dressed man named Benson—
in need of a shave; who it seemed no one barely knew—poured out his heart
to a stranger, because there had been no one else to tell.

⁂

He spoke about his wife Marga—who the year prior had died at forty-two;
a peasant girl from Hungary, he had met a dance, and held each night
until the end— the terrible years of sickness and decline, holding hope

doctor to doctor chasing cures; and how hard it had been
in the end when he could no longer care for her at home.

He told how he had been mostly working double shifts since at the plant—
seventy hours a week and sometimes more—having nothing else
to keep him apart from his loneliness.

⁂

All this though was long ago and now forgotten,
and these people, aside from the very youngest, are all gone too,
and their graves weather untended in toppled cemeteries along secondary roads.

Still, these disparate lives met one Sunday in a park in nineteen forty-seven,
and were invested, and presented themselves to photographer hired to hold the day

forever; wanting to be seen, and known, and remembered always,
for having lived, for having been here, and traveled there own internal worlds
filled with moments; albeit lives now past, and no longer really of consequence.

And later, that Sunday, after all but the very last had gone
and the sun began settling for the day,
while crickets began their nightly vespers:

buried stones—long cloistered in their scholared meditations
beneath the rye grass—pondered insights far greater than we can ever fathom;

and the long-fingered limbs of the giant evergreen
swayed in the passing breeze,
slowly, like the trunks of the great mastodons.

## THAT NIGHT

That night after we had walked up Broadway,
on the empty streets in the cold holding hands and talking
about this and that after having dinner at a friend's
where you said you maybe couldn't make it—
but had— for which I was so glad;

and after we had stopped by my place a few moments;
and had held each other and kissed again and again —gently,
then deep; and you made those murmur sounds you make
that come so soft from deep inside of you, even that first time,
on your street in front of your house

the night we met three weeks back, when I walked you
home through that beautiful snow the size of quarters;
we caught them on our tongues, and I carried your bag,
and felt in love, and so very glad about it all.
We stopped to watch the storm a for a while, under a sidewalk bridge,

as the snow hushed sounds that filled the city arm in arm with wonder,
went swirling gently past and haloed traffic lamps,
and everything felt as if it were inside one of those snow filled globes;
we wished each other Merry Christmas, pretending
and wishing it was, although it had been many weeks before.

That night at my place, I gave you those crystal earrings
from Ted Muehling's—that pretty shop at the end of Crosby—
I had bought on Valentine's Day;
I wanted to feel you were already my girlfriend,
but had become afraid, and been carrying them for days.

When you opened them, you said how they were like tiny icicles,
and I said yes, I had thought of that too when I bought them,
as a memory of that night we met, and the beautiful, beautiful snow;
you said it was dangerous to give someone a Valentine's,
and I said, that you could just pretend they were for Christmas.

Then we left, and I walked you towards your house,
a dozen blocks further on;  you said I didn't have to,
but it was nice of me to do. I told you, it was only because I wanted to,
and then you said, well, but that you said you wanted
to go the last few blocks alone.

I wrapped my arms around you again as we said goodnight on that corner
and you asked if I would be alright, if I'd miss you a lot until Sunday,
and that you had warned me it would be like this for a while;
I smiled and told you I would be OK; it was Tuesday night—
things were new—so Sunday night seemed very far away.

And there, out in the cold, in the pool of the streetlight lamp,
we held each other close, before you continued on alone.
I was very happy that we had met, and told you so,
and, you said yes, that you were happy too;
then—slowly across the frozen sidewalk— you disappeared into the dark.

THE LITTLE GIRLS:
THE EMPTY NEST

Those little girls are gone now
who once dressed for parties in velvet

dresses of foresty green and a bow tied in back
or burgundy or navy or black with a lace collar

and those blond bangs too are gone
and the rumpled tights

and the little shiny buckled shoes with straps
and their slippery too smooth soles

that clattered once as they danced  laughing
those Decembers on polished parquet floors.

MUTTON


Tonight, while I wait hopeful for an unlikely reply
    from a woman on an brown upholstered sofa—
300 miles away in Charlottesville, Virginia; holding a ukulele—

who I had emailed earlier in response to an on-line personal,
    where she describes herself as "a Middle Aged Naiad";
both of us it seems are searching pretty wide for affirmation.

Waiting, I think back again about an article I had read by R.W. Apple,
    earlier this week in the New York Times;
in life I am told he's known as Johnny, and is in fact quite a bear of a man.

The article espouses the joys of mutton as an unsung food;
    mostly I think of Fielding and Dickens, and remember eating it only once,
the certain summer when I was twenty, now over forty years ago.

It was the summer my friend Andy and I spent out west,
    on scholarships at an Art School in Aspen Colorado, back when
stray dogs still slept in warming puddles of sun, on the still unpaved streets.

We drove one weekend up to Wyoming to visit this famous sculptor
    we'd had known as a teacher, in Philadelphia the spring before.
He, David, was a wiry, leathered rail of a man with cold piercing eyes;

his sharp beak nose moved up and down when he spoke,
    in that voice yellowed from all those years of Gauloise that had stained
it, and two boney fingers on his right hand as well.

David spent his summers there on that arid *alta plana,*
    a lonely spot forty miles east of Cody along a dirt one lane road.
It was a place simply known to the Postal Service as, "via Cody, Wyoming",

a place roamed by tumbleweed and the wild horses,
    and his compound, just a small cluster of worn sod-roofed cabins
between the ragged mountains, and an ancient corral for the horses.

We got there, a while before twilight; soon after David arrived too,
    at full gallop on the back of a Palomino, raising dust with its hoof strikes
as it came to rest on that flat by the split-rail hitch.

Often, those summers, he would pass weeks at a time in the mountains;
    alone with a pack horse, carrying little more than his bow, a fishing rod,
a sack of flour or two, his bed-roll, and sometimes a rifle just in case.

For our dinner that evening there were mutton steaks—
    rough sawn, as if crosscut just earlier, fresh from a sheep's leg—
that David threw to the pinion coals in the hearth of the living room fire.

Later in that same room for entertainment after dinner,
    there would be shooting of handguns at the pack rats, as they ran
franticly through, between and over the rustic furnishings.

Enthralled , as the mutton steaks cooked buried in those embers—
    turned now and then to even the char— I sat, and in time I ate
silently from a worn tin plate—as best I could, dusting off the ash—
                              and trying to act as if I belonged,

That night crickets cried as a bazillion stars shown outside overhead;
    the only other sounds, aside from us, were the lonely wind, and the silence;
and the wild horses as they passed among the sage, miles and miles away.

# DREAMS

I wonder how it works in dreams, is there is some dramaturg in charge?
How skilled they must be to every night come up with all those metaphors,
assembled each day as they thumb their card catalogs
that require to be dutifully updated, so as to always select out a perfect choice
to be put up as the evening's performance.

I wonder too what crew of carpenters each day readies the scenery;
those labyrinthine venues, with secret passages;
resurrected houses and apartments you once lived in long ago,
who's keys the propman has silently slipped into your pocket without notice.
Familiar places, now somehow different, yet still filled with many things
                         you had meant to go back for, but somehow never did.

And where do they come from, those characters that you meet along the way,
those people who in fact mostly, you have never really met.
Where are they found, those faces; personae, culled from who knows where,
who when once fully costumed, seamlessly enter
to perform in their scenes so convincingly?

All so highly professional, these Lunts and Fontaines
from traveling troupes of vagabond players,
plying their trade, while wandering nightly mind to mind,
and each having likely first seen their lines that afternoon,
hours only before their one night run.

Hail to these rag-tag players, men and women of various age and stature,
who show up each day for the casting calls so enthusiastic,
wearing galoshes and worn knit caps. Happy, on even short notice,
to take the most demanding role in an evening's drama;
and to play parts, so often, of someone they appear nothing like.

I wonder where they go, the ones who play the perfect lovers
that hold so close in those moments before our waking,
and in the morning have always disappeared.
How careful they are not to leave a trace upon their departure;
never a single hair even, left among your night rumpled sheets.

## IN THE SUMMER OF 1949

In 1949 when I was four, and we spent our summer
    weekends, and a two week stretch mid-August, at the beach
out in West Hampton, with two light-dappled rooms
    my parents rented in the dormered upstairs
of a white clapboard farmhouse with a half-frayed clothesline,
    and a blue, four-door Plymouth coupe, parked by the screen porch door.

The kitchen had oil-cloth counters, and well-stocked shelves
    behind painted, glass-front wood cabinets doors;
the enamel table, with its three mismatched chairs, always
    waited centered, on the languid linoleum floor, and the rich smells
mixed with nutmeg, that lasted on from years of Sundays,
    and of rolled out pie-crust, and white flour turned with yeast.

Herb Culver, fourth generation duck farmer, had been born in that house;
    had seen the droughts and hurricanes, and loved to tell the tales.
But after "The War", as land speculators began to arrive, top down
    in white-walled bright colored phaetons, Herb had feared for the future
of small family-run operations; around him others were shutting down.
    Times had changed; at age fifty-six, Herb began a new life as a plumber.

He outfitted the farm's old dark-green panel truck
    with shelves and bins to store the multitude of varied fitting—
all sizes of elbows, gate valves and a range of reduction unions—
    and on the roof, he fashioned a simple homemade rack
to hold strapped lengths of copper, and the greasy threaded pipe
    for shingled cottages, and soon coming Modern beach-front properties.

Friday nights we would drive out through the Midtown Tunnel,
    and make our way along Queens Boulevard, to the Northern State,
As we sang, top down, in that powder blue, chrome-grill Oldsmobile;
    the only car my father ever owned. In time the large roads gave way
to numbered two-lane blacktop through small towns with billboards,
    and saloons with neon flashing lights to entice the passing stranger.

Later, there'd be the loving farms
    with their white roadside stands, selling in season—
pies, and corn and tomatoes—
    and then as the sun would start to set, and the crickets begin,
somewhere past Lake Ronkonkoma,
    I would fall to sleep.

After breakfast, on those next sea-breeze mornings long ago,
    once more, top down, we made our way past the rustling salt marsh cattails
along the sand strewn asphalt causeway, to Rodgers Beach
    across the channel drawbridge—
as the gulls and billowed sailboats would make their way as well—
    and there as we would change to our bathing suits; me, so awkwardly.

We would stand, me and my Dad, in that men's locker room—
    with its slatted benches and cold salty showers; he and I at our rented locker
that had hooks on the wall, and a little wooden door that locked
    with a brass numbered key— and I would compare myself
to the muscled, sun-browned men, across the wide wood-planked floor;
    the floor, still so cool those mornings from the prior evening mist;

then so hot in the late afternoon from hours of the day's sun burning down.
    Once ready we gathered our terrycloth towels and the bag with his cameras,
and be off then to spend those long hours on the white sand beyond;
    down the worn wood weather-beaten stairs, and past the dune grass,
to only just halfway to crashing ocean's shore; and there to lay,
    slathered in Skol or Tar-tan, as it seemed to aid our bronzing in the sun.

There, each day as I sat waiting for something more,
    and the green bottle-flies bit, and sand crabs skittered by
while I built my lonely sandcastles, as the sun beat harshly down,
    and be warned about the undertow, how lurked invisibly beyond
I would wonder about the ocean, could I see perhaps to the other side;
    and if one day when I was big, would I maybe fly off to the stars?

Even then—albeit secretly—I worried a lot about death;
  about life and time, growing old and other fearful scenerios.
Too afraid to ask, or say a word, for fear of them all coming too soon true;
  for diversion, I'd walk silently alone along the sand collecting;
continuum of rusted bottle caps, sea glass and pearlescent mussel shells;
  treasure to take home and to keep for forever, in a sandy paper-bag.

And then, now and again, holding to grown-up's hand uneasily,
  I'd stand a while in that froth of the shore-wash breakers,
as the tide washed sand would slide so mysteriously
  out from underneath my feet as I stood, and dizzy my balance;
and the seabirds, they would call out in such acheful cries as they looped—
  it seemed as if —so endlessly overhead.

## WAITING OUT THE RAIN

"No", said the young pretty Asian girl with tattoos,
to the handsome dayshift manager at the tapas bar in Chelsea,
        as I sat nursing a glass of wine

before my friend Jessica's opening;
killing time (not wanting to arrive too early)
        and waiting out the rain.

"No", she said,
seemingly trying to clarify
        (the manager himself still only a kid)

"I leave for LA on the eighth",
and then, a little later,
        "or maybe I'll go to Las Vegas."

For modern travelers (meeting at crossroads waiting for Godot)
none of these sorts of temporal things,
        at this point really matter anymore.

VESPER

I had driven up the road at twilight towards the beaver pond,
where a school of ducks were nestled into the upper cove
it seemed they were bedding down for the evening,
headed south no doubt; a little late it seemed, it being already November,
but then autumn has been lingering on this year.
They were all faced the same direction, as if some ritual reverie,

or in evening prayers perhaps, towards the setting sun;
as it lands this time of year behind that distant ridge.
It brought to mind a week ago Sunday in Prospect Park
with you and the light that then had seemed so much the same.
We had talked about the early darkening—about seasons, and rituals,
and there had been then too, an adoration for the moment—as we passed
        among the clusters of others on our way
                back towards Flatbush, brushing shoulders now and then.

You had taken me to see that special tree, where you had made a shrine
for your parents, and would come to from time to time;  you said,
aside from your son there were not a lot of others you had not brought there,
and how you had dug in the trodden soil at its base, to place a small Buddha—
you said—a blue marble, and some other few things I can't remember;
I felt very privileged you had brought along.

I watched as you knelt to clear the dirt between the gnarled trunk roots, sprung
in open clefs above the ground, and spend your moment like a shaman, quietly.
You showed me too the weathered penny you had left to always mark the spot,
entrusting it as the guardian—raised it, turned it twice, and put it back—
and then you stood, and we walked out again into the grass,
from under the low-spreading autumn canopy, and that was that.

I asked if you knew what sort of tree it was, you said didn't,
and then if I could  take a leaf, because I didn't either— wanting:
to remember the time, and look it up, so I could tell you
and gain your love—you said it was OK,
and so I chose one I thought unlikely to be missed;
it all seemed so very special, and then slowly we moved on.

And so now here upstate where I have come alone
to do the end of summer chores—to bring the cordwood in,
and bed the gardens down mulched deep in leaves raked off the front lawn,
as the brown begins, and the thistle turn to white and wispy seed; I wish
I had brought that leaf along with me, to look up and have the good excuse to call
you—as the ladybugs seek their winters refuge too, in the early twilight—now

        when the last pale lilac wisps of the day fade at the horizon,
        and the vegetable stew simmers slow on the kitchen stove.

## SUNSHINE SEEMS THE CLOSEST THING I HAVE EVER KNOWN TO GOD

O to those first silk smooth days when
sunlight warm wraps like newly ironed sheets,
and the morning air tastes sweet of lychees;
O to the fresh breathed rays that finger through—

cleansing, and restoring a sense of hopefulness—
laying upon the city's sidewalk, as they do,
on first turned fields soon to be growing,
and the dew damp lawns, raising fresh mown scents,
                        that linger long past their last cutting,

and to the glints and glistens that play
from each leaf's whisperings
of the curbside ginkgos
wavering in some gentle passing on.

And O too, to the young woman who steps
lively along on the early morning sidewalk;
light catches the soft of a just showered shoulder,
and rounds her muscled calf with the dream of a summer's tan.

The rayon polka-dotted dress sashays
a counterpoint to the song of her hips, as she passes,
with the sound of clattering heels as she disappears,
off to her nine-to-five on this late April morning;

as I return from the store, having only gone
to buy some milk for my morning tea,
yet now, somehow, everything now has changed,
from only just moments prior.

## WOMAN AT THE FRONT DESK OF THE CANDLE-LITE MOTEL

The woman at the front desk that night of the Candle-Lite Motel
   had drawn him in like a moth into another bright a lit fantasy,
a world where he goes to all too often now these days, and dreams
   of lithe gentle women he has seen now and then—slender, caring women
in slips of cotton dresses; satin skinned and hard upturn-nippled as mannequins—
   and in those dreams, a mutually unfaultable love is at long last finally found.

Maybe this time it was just the lust of that umber lipstick, that taken him on to there,
   or the musty rumpled scent of her deep-red gypsy hair;
but there had to be seemed more as he checked-in, late, after that sultry August rain.
   That evening there had been a wordless wanting he felt, that came
from her lined, dark full-pupiled eyes; a beckoning etched from hard times,
   like the women in Raymond Carver stories.

She wears a small gold cross which hangs off a tiny latched link-chain,
   that drapes languid across her collarbones, and the pale
of the blouse covered flesh. The chain glows green in the fluorescent light
   hung from overhead, as soulful rhythm seep from the AM radio
she has tuned to the Pentecostal station; late at night on a road between two places;
   one he had left, that morning, the other still yet to be found.

Thought the man knows too well, that dreams will only come true in dreams,
   later, as he lays longing— alone, in his rented room in the dark; curtains drawn—
he seeks meaning, and endlessly dismisses the impossibilities as he weaves
   elaborate scenarios out of intuited wisps, and shadows of wished for innuendo;
wanting so to believe that this time it could all be different,
   were he only to go back for some ice perhaps, or to ask for another towel.

And so that night, at the Candle-Lite Motel as the man sleeps fitfully
   on the too wide bed alone— and his wife sleeps too, and his children,
in that silent house he had left at sunrise, now hundreds of miles away—
   he dreams, and an ebb of white clouds slowly cross the waning moon,
as night creatures roam the unfamiliar landscape,
   and cicadas sing to their longing love song the stars.

And in his dreams that night as he sleeps,
   all is warm and spring; and in his garden there are flowers blooming
past the stonewall, beyond the potentilla—
   new ones that he has never had, and yet has wanted for so long—
swarms and swarms of blue hydrangea
   blossoming; there where it had always been impossible before.

## THE NIGHT BEFORE, THE WEATHER RADIO FORECAST RAIN

Sitting alone by an early morning fire, in the half dark
and airless sounds, only days before the end of summer;
wind waves clatterings of pelting rain across a metal farmhouse roof
and insects hide in burrows hoping for safety,

not knowing what else to do; you watch the giant full-leafed maple
limbs voicelessly rise and settle softly outside the kitchen window, and know
they too will soon now be gone, and so much looms
that already has secretly begun.

It had all seemed so impossible the night before
when the weather radio forecast rain—
after a day that had been so beautiful; and the sunset
more humbling than any in such a long, long time—

funny sometimes how the world can just turn on a dime.

ON THAT TUESDAY MORNING


On that Tuesday morning,
trees grew infinitesimally closer to the winter
that seemed that clear Indian summer day, so very distant still.

Bread lay in the bakery windows waiting;
sidewalks were swept;
birds rested perched on the city's limestone ledges.

That Tuesday morning, lovers awoke among their twisted sheets:
showered, dressed—spoke of later on—
and coffee was made unmindfully.

People went to work and the children were sent to school.
By 8:42—as the freshly swept sidewalks once again began collecting dust—
the balance had shifted in an instant, and everything became different for always.

Most of all now still, when I think of those early moments,
it is of those who chose—facing irrefutable truth; knowing it their only option—
that they, like winged angels perhaps, might too be able to fly.

SOAP

Sometimes, we will hold to the tiniest wisp of something
that feels imbued with memory; a touchstone that provides
us safety— or love, or hope, or wealth —
and so we keep as a secret friend.


Perhaps some special ribbon, or meaningless matches from somewhere long ago,
still we protect and parse them out for years, as dearly as we might
the final foil-wrapped slice of wedding cake, or the last of Christmas cookies,
secreted in a painted tin, where we dare rarely more than a stolen glimpse.


It could only be a lonely wafer of soap we impose our investment in;
a gift from a lover once, perhaps, or then again maybe not
laying among others, uneasily, in its reliquary along the bathtub rim,
half translucent with edges worn sharp as a cuttlebone blade;


a slip of soap—in truth saved now for nothing more, than simply saving's sake—
we watch each night as we soak—making plans, or reflecting on events of the day,
while imagined crosswords weave amid the grouted tile—
and weigh if tonight maybe, we deserve to use a little more.


Still we hold to these cherished nothings dearly—
as if the sun's last corn-stubbled rays in a late October,
crossing hay in a bale full field—or the shards of love,
long after the impossibilities have become known—
                    fearful that another spring never again may come.

## NOW, AND WITH THE SUMMER ALMOST GONE

They tell him down at the farm equipment place in town,
  his thirty year old yard tractor has gotten where it's foolish to repair.
They say it will be close to five-hundred dollars maybe more, probably,
  and then who knows what might be next. He hates to let it go,
                    after all the time there had been.

It's hard to face how nothing lasts forever, to accept the inevitable,
  that past a certain point, things aren't worth holding on to anymore.
They'll give him a good trade-in on a new John Deere, they say;
  he hurts to know that likely at his age, it is the last he gets to buy.
                    There are many ways to measure time.

Some days, aside from chores, he feels he's not good for much anymore.
  Often they are easier to deal with, and so he tries to make them feel important.
The hard work tires him, and the aches make him feel he got something done.
  He worries that too soon he won't be able to,
                    and then what will happen to it all.

Some days he will wander inside straightening, wanting to put things right.
  Recently he read a book of poems by Ginger Andrews; they reminded him
of a woman, and that no doubt, she would have liked them too.
  He wishes he would not still think of what might please her,
                    how now he has done that for way too long a time.

On the way that he drives to his daughter's friend, there is a hundred year old willow
  he loves, at the bend on the quiet road. There is a quiet timelessness of there—
as if in early landscape paintings—and of the tree— with its long twisted branches
  in windblown towerings and half-still wisps of leaves—
                    so imbued with god and grandeur.

It seems so wise and tranquil, in spite of all the years of harshness it has seen,
  secreted away in that field with the weathered split rail fence,
and the green shingled slope-roofed shed beyond that glimmers dappled
  in the coming August twilight,
                    that tonight he wishes he could share with someone.

On the way home after shopping at the Grand Union, he notices
    the maples here and there, have already begun to turn at their edges.
That new cashier had just flirted with him some, he thought,
    then thinks about it again, as he drives home through the shafting twilight,
                        and how maybe he could ask her out sometime.

He thinks how he could take her to dinner one night after she was off from work;
    that new place one town over, as the sun was heading down.
He would wear his ironed khakis, he imagines, and that white fresh-folded shirt;
    and she, a pretty cotton dress, and they would laugh.

                    He would tell her about the willow tree;
                    and they'd touch hands gently across the table.

These days, he wonders about life's roads: what lies beyond forks,
    and how there won't be second chances on them anymore.
And so now the darkness rolls in, and the fear of heading somewhere
    he doesn't want to go — as the blackberries pass
                        and with the summer almost gone.

*TOM CORBETT, SPACE CADET: LOS ANGELES MAY 17 2006 (AP)—*

*Frankie Thomas, who starred in the 1950's television show "Tom Corbett, Space Cadet", died here on Thursday. He was 85.*

*At his request, Mr. Thomas was buried Tuesday in his "Tom Corbett, Space Cadet" costume.*

## ON APRIL TWENTY-NINTH

On April twenty-ninth, the sun already sets past eight.
Three months from now I will start to forage dinner from the garden;
another three, and once more all of that will end.

Kunitz speaks of the importance of death; the catastrophe—he says—
of accumulation that would come upon us, were it not in place;
yet for me I think there are things that should just go on forever.

In time I wonder what they all will say about me— perhaps the truth;
that he did a lot of things pretty good, and nothing all that well;
and will they play for me as requested, a Bach cello suite, and a little Marvin Gaye?

I hope they mention how so he loved his children, and longed only after simple joys:
making things, and growing gardens, the beautiful mountains, and billowed clouds;
sunsets; the smell of a barn; garlic, red wine, and a gentle woman's touch.

Will they say: how he loved to cook for friends, and how so often that he had;
that he mowed his lawns, tidied the house, and always tried make things more
beautiful, in hope of being loved; and that sentimental movies made him cry?

Now and then, I will pass an old tattersalled man on the street,
and know that he remembers: two girls, one summer once—
one in shorts, and the other in a cotton dress—

and how the sun, it had shown so intently then
that afternoon, on the smooth of their just washed skin;
and how they had passed, and that they had smelled so very sweetly.

## THERE WAS SOMETHING IRREVOCABLE

There had been something irrevocable about the way she said *we* that morning
    on the phone, as he stood there in the chill of his half-light kitchen
    with a cup of tea, and the cold receiver held against his ear; it was early,
    he had been up for hours, but had not yet dressed for the day.

It was the particular *we*—referring to herself and the man she had left him for,
    by then already six years past, and really two and a half more
    if you count the time they still stayed together,
    for next to no reason, as it seemed it had turned out—

a *we,* that made the worn cotton threads he clung to, —
    wanting to believe somehow there would still be a reversal:
    that it all had been a mistake; that it was only a test of his fortitude,
    and that sun-patched fields of unending glory were soon to open,
        and they would join hand in hand again, for ever and ever,
        as he had always known it would be—

seem then all the less realistic; and yet, he somehow still finds miraculous ways.

EVEN NOW (THE RING)

Even now, once in a while when his thumb might stroke absentmindedly down
and across the vacancy where the wedding ring once had anchored him;

        sometimes for a pale green moment he will wonder
nervously, where he might have mislaid it,
missing it—like a phantom limb—suddenly as if only for the first time;

        startled after all these years,
            when the callous ridge it made is finally all but gone.

ROADS

There was this piece in the paper today about perinatal deaths.
It spoke of how— having nothing to do with religion—the parents—
knowing their future child will die unborn, or perhaps only hours after birth—
still carry their baby to term, just because they simply feel they have to,
and how for so many, there feels just no other choice

The piece spoke of the desperation with which these parents care;
how they cradle their naked children on their chest—dead or alive—
confess the darkest of intimacies— in hope of some small redemption—
and to build family memories in whatever way they can;
roads will often bring us places unimaginable to withstand.

There is a strip of elevated highway I see driving south
on I-95 not far outside of Richmond. It seems as just a ribbon
balanced barely on spindly sticks; I am glad I have never had to drive it—
it has always seemed just too frightening, too perilous—
though roads, I know, can feel less threatening when you are riding on them.

I had a dream the other night, in it I was driving. At a certain point
I found myself towards dusk, lost in a small town somewhere;
in a working neighborhood, in someone's driveway, at the end of a winding road.
It was just a quiet place, nothing special, but I felt it kind of frightening;
I knew I didn't belong there, and needed to quickly turn around.

The house was a simple single-story white clapboard, built in the 1950's maybe,
and in the yard, a black man my age in overalls who lived there
and seemed probably always had. Likely there were things we might have had
to talk about, things in common, things we might have found to shared;
but I was glad I was able to turn around quickly, thankful I hadn't come in a truck.

    There are ends to roads, I guess, where people must spend entire lives;
    places just too small to turn around in, and go another way.

## LAR BARGSTED

There had been an early chill that September morning,
when Lar padded the furnished apartment floor, before
he heading off to work five miles south in Sutter Falls.

After High School, and two years in the service abroad,
Lar Bargsted, answering a random want-ad; settled in Braxton,
and has been working over at Dugan's, in the office mostly, ever since.

At Dugan's, Lar looks after their orders, does the payroll, the books,
and aside from a bowling league, twice a month in season,
has always pretty much just kept to himself.

Later though, on that one, star-filled, end of summer night—
as the clouds passed over the half-full moon,
ebbing with nearly painful translucency—

Lar Bargsted, age at 53, rose in his sprawled, dark worsted suit
to fold his worn wooden chair, after everyone else had gone on
home from that last of the season's band concerts on the village green;

and, almost teary eyed, was seen heading breathless
toward the Grange Hall, and its part-tuned upright piano,
for reasons he could not truly put his finger on,

having never felt the calling before,
but now, somehow, overcome suddenly
with an aching need to sing.

His thinning hair lay plastered to his broad sweated brow, as he walked on—
so purposefully in those worn brown wingtip broughams
that had so long since been in need of fresh half soles—
                    fervent in his hope of finding someone to chord along.

## THE OTHER NIGHT

Lying there the other night next to you
naked asleep in your loft bed
with that map of Texas next to us on the wall—

sleepless after making love
after the dinner you had made, and the talk we had—
listening to the street sounds and the silence,

and the thrum and slur of the oscillating fan
on the kitchen floor a room away.
          There half buried in the tangled sheets

I felt so glad to be next to you
still in spite of everything,
or maybe in truth it was only just because.

A ROMANCE (working title)


Yesterday, headed home once more cross-state along the Southern Tier;
    driving past long since fallen mill towns—their rust stained smoke-stack industry,
    no more now than the outskirts of a freshly minted mall—
    and hundred acre farms—some still worked with an aging tractor,
    though many more abandoned, their homestead overgrown, or nothing perhaps,
        but a tiled silo maybe still remaining.


The world was so richly thick in mid-September opulence—now
    barely a week before the start of Fall; and all so beautiful,
    under ebbing skies—the endless swelling clouds shifting
    mile after mile transfixing me for hours as I drove—
    through violent storm and clearing—along the flats, and dappled hills
        broad coursed with winding rivers.


Glorious pastorals, balance on swelling knife-edge asymmetries;
    adagios in dizzying color from grey to viridian and acid edged celadons—
    teals and ceruleans—and unnamed hues of vibrancy beyond all ever known.
    On and on those morphing pictures flowed, through the likes of Tiepolo—
    Bierstadt, Thomas Cole, and Martin Johnson Heade—and all then so very real,
        and far too impossible in truth, to really ever put down.

I REMEMBER MY MOTHER AT NINETY-THREE OFTEN SAYING
IN THOSE FINAL MONTHS BEFORE SHE DIED THAT MAYBE
SOMETIMES A PERSON JUST LIVES TOO LONG:
CANTATA AT AGE SIXTY; APRIL 2005

During that last week before the '04 the election last November,
I rode a bus out to Cleveland, with a bunch of others, hoping to try to help;
going door-to-door to talk to people, and drag them to the polls if necessary.

We spoke to poor and working-class people mostly, they understood
their vote could tip things to make a change, and though the change didn't come,
I feel good that I went, and it still seems it was the right thing to do.

In those heady grey November days by the fog wrapped shores of Lake Erie—
when we had our high hope, and still believed it would happen somehow—
we drove again and again past those empty steel mills;

all so sadly abandoned now and the weed sprouted parking fields beyond,
where once each day men arrived with lunch pails to work in the colossi of noise
and smoke inside those giant sheds, where for years they had no longer come.

The rusted blast furnaces, too sat so silently to pit and decay,
there amid the open rib-webbed buildings, corroding in the acid rain;
their iron grids of window sash, filled with only cobwebs and shattered glass.

***

Driving north last week with my younger daughter to Geneseo, NY
to visit a college she will likely be off to in the fall;
I found myself wondering, yet again, where the world was going.

For six hours we rode along interstates, where only a milk road once wound its way
slowly along the southern tier not that long ago; on it rolled to Rochester,
past hill-town farms, through villages with hand-pump filling stations—
a café, a store—and a small white shingled church.

Here and there we passed the faded patchwork farms that had been so proud—
a Ford 8N tractor still tilling the fields, and its barns added to in oddly fashioned ways
as needs arose—and last lone diners, that each town once had one of;

clapboard motels with names like, Cozy Rest, and The Starbrite Inn,
that now sit so discarded along the sides of the cracked macadam off-ramp spurs,
at the edge of shuttered town; their vacancy signs lit pointlessly as they wait.

Once proud towns where dormer gingerbread lingers only in a random here and there,
and the front-porch fretwork rots slowly, like sad splayed tooth pumpkins
on worn wooden steps, two weeks past a rained-out Halloween.

I honor all those last traces I see of forgotten hope-filled enterprise, begun after the
war, and their once bright futures that now have past: empty mills, and discarded
factories— now gone, or grown and moved to places very far away—

the remains of older refineries;
chemical, and fertilizer plants, with rusted tanks of such seemingly random size,
as if each was once bought from some passing salesman, long ago on a whim;

and abandoned anthracite mines, with their tipples,
and viaducts corroding; and then later, at sunset, a rock-salt operation,
working still, and seeming to be making a go of it all somehow.

And yes too, to those railroad bridges that I love, where trains now no longer run—
their arced iron trusses in half collapse, and stone laid footings,
holding strong to the thick clear current's frothing.

Those tributaries, surging now from the spring snow melt;
streams and rivers roiling brown—the Delaware and the beautiful Susquehanna—
and soon their backwater washes will fill with full chorus of the teeming peepers' cry.

We drive, past mammoth malls, filled each day with countless swarms; country lives,
once built on independence, who now find safe comfort in uniformity—chains stores,
and fast food restaurants, each one is always just the same—and there again I wonder;

in times to come, will this not too be but romantic memory to be longed for;
and then, who will there be to watch all that that I have so loved, in early Aprils,
as the forsythia bud, and turn to their abundant bloom.

\*\*\*

There was a community sing at my younger daughter's school, this afternoon
commemorating the life of Charity Bailey, a former music teacher,
who when I was a kid I had semi-known, but now dead almost thirty years.

It felt good walking over, the sky a crisp wide cloud-wisped blue—
with one cumulonimbus,, that lay like a favorite sweater rumpled near the horizon—
and the air smelled laced with promise, then, as I sauntered slowly on my way.

Sadly though, the songs they sung sounded different from the way we learned them—
And though I tried to let it pas it seemed as if somehow with these new people singing,
that in truth the songs were not fully felt or perhaps really understood.

It turned out, Pete Seeger had come too, to pay honor to Charity,
though at first I hadn't recognized it was him sitting silent near the rear;
an awkward white-haired old man with an instrument case, wearing an orange knit cap.

On the last song, "Passing Through", he strode haltingly to the front, banjo in hand
to frail along. I wanted to tell him, it had been him, the first time music made me cry
—him at Carnegie Hall, him; as he had played, "Bells of Rhymney", on a twelve-string.

I had been fifteen, that April night, and sat alone in last row of the top balcony,
with the plays of Garcia Lorca in the pocket of my blue corduroy jacket,
back when it seemed there was so much yet still to come.

That late spring night, how much I wanted someday be like him, and wanted
for so many things as I stroked the carved scroll of the wooden armrest
awkwardly, and fingered the red velvet upholstery, fore and against the grain.

## AT THE ICE CREAM PARLOUR

When he was small, in solitude, the boy might be taken, so as to comfort on hot summer day afternoons, down the block to eat ice cream out of small silvered bowls. Silently, there the boy sits; private thoughts come to him from the territories, among the small hexagonals on the worn tile floor. There are areas he must turn away from. They make him ache, & those he does not return to; the messages are all too clear; patterns mean different things. Secretly his hand wanders below the table, tracing a swale on the rough enamel-painted wall. His forefinger lingers at the berm of a crack long since re-plastered; a fly enters through a tear in the front-door screen. Want is criminal—thoughts—clamps must keep them. He knows he must be careful; everywhere there are watching eyes. On the sidewalk a woman in a felt hat passes; her seamed stockings move up her muscled calf, slowly like a razor's scar. The pock-faced waitress in a starched white uniform, reaches into eight-lid freezer behind the counter, her smooth veined arm deep goes into darkness beyond where he can see. Reaching again and again with the raw metal scoop, her uniform buttons strain against her flesh. He watches. It embeds in him. Louder now, the pendulum clock slowly ticks. The boy rests the round back of the cold spoon gently for a moment against the top welt of his upper lip; then, hard, he presses, its sharpened edge in. It is the afternoon; the boy sits alone. In the ice cream parlour, the wooden radio rests silent on the oil-cloth bracket shelf. His small marble table is shadowed by the overhead fan. On the sawdust, on the patched tile floor, the wire, ribbed-wood seated chair fingertips; back and forth, looking for balance. Each day women pass like a torn shooting gallery. One-by-one their stain imbedded him. Once weekly with a long brass key, the pendulum clock is rewound.

CROSSING THE SUSQUEHANNA

The Susquehanna is such a beautiful river as it rolls,
headwaters to basin, endlessly confirming life's continuums
with a humble authority unquestionable as Mahalia Jackson.

There is a particular crossing I love along I-95,
just west of Harve de Grace, that I always look forward to passing,
and yet each time it takes me by surprise.

There is a quiet majesty there, that overshadows all distraction;
an elegiac, imposing beauty—wonder filled as Bierstadt, Kensett,
and Thomas Eakins—that implodes all sense of time.

I pointed the place out last week to my older daughter as we drove,
taking her back to North Carolina for her second year away at school;
she probably didn't see what I tried to show her, yet I really hoped she could.

I want her to know how glory can show in simple moments, and be
powerful enough to transcend all time, and to quiet everything
at least for a while; it was just that gift I wanted to pass along.

At that crossing when you look upriver to the west,
the deep channels show darkened in the water, marking
paths the buckskin flatboat-traders once traveled laden—

with bundled beaver pelts and provisions— as they wove
their way through islands and oxbows,
along the wide set banks deep forested in primeval oak and evergreen.

Downriver to the east, the quarried palisade, still so alive with machinery,
and beyond, the arced railroad bridges, of long bowed iron truss.
Homage to mythic America; romance, of shirtsleeves rolled high;

homage to veined forearms of working men at the end of a long July day;
homage to hope, and lazier times that seem to be no more; times we still believed in
only if, and that the world could be beautiful always.

I'd crossed there too in 1964 when I was still in Art School,
driving south for a weekend in Baltimore; to visit Sue and Scott,
and help fix up the house they had only just bought.

Scott was in the service then, and the war was grinding on.
Viet Nam was mostly all I thought about in those days;
each time I heard a plane overhead, it made me so afraid.

The year before, after Kennedy was shot, I'd hitched down too
to Washington with Shelly. We stood in-line all night with all those others,
and then at dawn we walked past the shrouded coffin in the Capital Rotunda.

Silently there for a moment in the blinding glare of TV lights—
the still honor guard waiting like wax figures; with helmets and rifles steadied —
after a sleepless night; an hour later, we hitch-hiked home.

In those backseats of rides that morning, I rested my head uncertainly
on Shelly's shoulder— lost in what all had happened, and all that yet might be—
and we touched thigh to thigh, as we longed now for finding any comfort.

In 1964 in Baltimore, afternoon sun glittered off the paint-blistered storefronts
of neighborhood street-corner markets; and through dusty-plate glass windows,
warming the five-cent bags of Lay's potato chips that hung beyond,

on rusting metal racks the white-aproned shopkeepers refilled fresh
each day. The turnover was brisk there in those poorer neighborhoods;
we all must our find comfort where we can.

And so we sat there, me and my friends, that first afternoon at start of autumn,
each with our own bag, on their worn-out three-step limestone stoop.
And there, as the sun began to fall, nothing really has ever been much better.

IN MEMORIAM


Last Friday at the county hospice in Kingston,
Edie Jensen— almost eighty-three— was still smiling when
I brought her roses, and we held each other's hand—
the I-V connected to the other—for most of the hour or so, I was there.

Two nights before, Linda, her older daughter, had called;
Edie, she said, was getting moved the next day from St. Benedict's;
I had not known that she was sick; I would stop to visit her
three or four times a year, but I hadn't been in a while.

Needless to say, I am very glad I got there, that rainy Friday afternoon,
and that we had some time to chat, as she drifted in and out of the morphine;
across the room— surrounded in stuffed animals— the roommate watched
Dr. Phil on a wall-mounted TV.

"Come on," Edie said, at one point off-handedly,
opening those sunken eyes, and tightening the hold she held on my hand—
she looked so terribly old, and somehow yet still pretty at the same time—
"Come on", she said, "Let's just get out of here and get a drink".

Saturday, I began turning my vegetable garden early; 24x36, seven small raised beds.
Later, just needing to—looking for hope I suppose—I planted a few packets of seeds.
A row or two each of spinach, snow peas, and Swiss chard;
just ones that can stand hard frost, since certainly there was more still to come.

Monday evening, Linda phoned again: Edie, she said had died on Sunday;
"slipped away", she said, "not long after you had left"; and so that, I guess, was that.
Edie, and Norman her husband, they had always been my benchmarks, my ideals.
That will likely remain so always; they were what I hold everyone up to, to measure.

As a child I could see the Empire State Building from my bedroom window.
Just recently, I found it was built only thirteen years before I was born;
it still seems pretty hard to believe. I had assumed it was there much longer;
it is far too important to have begun only so close to me.

## WOODPECKERS

Woodpeckers, I was reading somewhere the other day,
do not actually have a song, and so they use their beaks,
not just to gather food, but as noisemakers, desperate to be noticed—
asserting self-importance, to overcome their insecurity—
                        and like so many of us, in hope of finding love.

Today upstate, I strung the Christmas lights up early,
before I went on about my other chores. I scalloped them, as always,
across the front porch fascia, making sure that the wires come out even
to spiral, like a barber's pole, down the outside lathe-turned columns;
                        it seems safest to have everything ready now, just in case.

Dutifully I raked the front lawn leaves, and brought the firewood in;
and the summer gardens I laid in mulch, so as to be safely bedded down for winter.
And now through driveway meadows, the apples all have fallen,
littering their winter browse around the twisted trunks,
                        so purposeful in their random disorder.

Silently now I wait in those twilights when the days are short and lightly ambered;
watching as the sun clings close to the leafless tree horizons,
and wonder about purpose, and what else yet there is to come.
And the apples, they must wait too, beneath the trees in the darkness;
                        patiently for the coming of a passing deer.

CAPS

Autumn afternoons, when the boy was five, or almost six,
    he spent alone. In a room with the blue painted walls, abandoned
        fire trucks lay in disarray at the bottom of his wooden chest.

In those fading afternoons, a fly might have settled now and then
    on the windowsill, as sun slid through the lowered Venetian blinds,
        patterning slatted lines across the dark squares of the parquet floor.

Secretly once—the boy, being resourceful—tried to make caps
    for the silver cowboy pistol; he cut paper strips he crayoned red,
        and then applied black dots at what had seemed the proper spacings.

When they did not work, he felt great fear and guilt over what he had done:
    he tried to cheat, tried to fool them; taken shortcuts, and been far to careless.
        They had not been drawn well enough, he had avoided the more difficult work.

The boy was almost six already; he knew better, knew he had to work harder,
    and understood, though the blinds were lowered, the judges still had watched.
        Punishment would come in time; it had all been seen, and it made him afraid.

DEAR P

It's pretty nice here P, what with the blue-sky spring just beginning;
earlier I had a wood-fire, but now—outside in only a t-shirt—
   the world is warm, and the trees wait for their leaves impatiently.

No, since you ask, things here are not yet exactly "green",
most remains patched with snow, the rest just brown and muddy.
   At the moment, my yard, in truth, seems more a marsh than a lawn;

it is rutted deep in the aftermath of the winter's plowings—and driving in-and-out
last week and this, has also made more work for me to do—
   and yet it feels so good, to sense what in time it will all again become.

Now while snowdrops lay clustered under trees,
the jonquil blades prepare for their first honey-scented flowerings;
   and below the house, the frenzied stream roils, carrying away winter's grey remains.

Earlier today I gathered the heavy downed branches along the driveway windbreak;
long-needled evergreens, snapped in the weight of a late wet snow
   two weeks back;

and I cleared the culverts, and hoed fresh channels to focus the rambling watercourses
that wander the meadows now, everywhere it seems;
   my gardens, for a while yet I fear, will be impossible to turn.

So no, no peepers, at least not yet; I think it's still way too cold;
but my-o-my, P, last night the sky;
   it was truly filled with stars, and very, very humbling.

## HEADING WEST IN THE ODDLY MILD JANUARY

Heading west in the grey of drizzle, along route 17
as it follows the course of the winding Susquehanna past fallow fields,
unblemished still for another 50 miles, by even the smallest patches of snow.
We stopped for a bit, my daughter and I, to buy gas and to take a rest

at the truck stop near Kanona, NY; a space station along the highway;
and I no more than another traveler in this earthly galaxy.
We were heading to her to college south of Rochester;
a few days early after the winter break.

Inside, steaming Silex pots fog the stainless steel behind the service counter,
as the middle-aged waitresses on a weekend shift, dream of another life perhaps,
refilling the emptied mugs endlessly—in their bleached hair, and too-tight uniforms—
and call all the traveling strangers, "doll", in hope of better tips.

In that giant white-lined parking lot beyond the herded rows of silenced
diesel semi's—Freightliners and Peterbilts; their drovers asleep
in the musty berths behind the cabs, alone and far from home—
were two small horse-drawn carriages.

Two Amish wagons, side by side, so seemingly out of place.
Simple black wooden boxes, with spoked, steel-rimmed wheels,
hitched with small, matted brown horses, standing steady;
their heads down-thrust in resignation, to the soft misting rain.

Standing at the gas pumps, having just refilled my tank,
I saw five the Amish boys coming toward me from very far away.
They strode synchronously in their chambray shirts, and suspendered
woolen trousers, like a long lens shot out of a Terrence Malleck movie;

each with a quart-sized soda in their hand, from the Subway franchise.
They laughed and sipped now and then as they walked along, in those hard straw hats;
posturing in their rag-tag way— as might any other group of teenaged boys
with longings—out for a prowl on a Saturday afternoon.

As the boys came closer—preparing, I assumed, to sit finish their drinks,
and then just continue uneventfully on their way, back to wherever
it was from which they had come, that drizzly afternoon—I could see,
that an older Plymouth sedan had since pulled up to the parking slot next to theirs.

We drove past them on our way back to the highway; the Plymouth
passengers, five high school girls, alone and primped for the afternoon.
They all just sat there with their longings, it seemed, locked, behind invisible barriers;
wanting, but not daring yet, to throw all caution to the wind.

I wondered later how it all turned out: if in time was there contact made,
and for a while at least, had they walked off hand-in-hand into the silvered clouds?
Have we not all had our desperate longings for fresh starts and happy endings,
impossibilities that transcend our daily lives, and so who are we to say.

What gloried wonders might have passed there
that afternoon—albeit words, perhaps, were never spoken—
and what secret dreams will now lay wound with them forever,
cloistered, late at night, among their twisted sheets.

## A POEM ON MY MOTHER'S DYING

For Christmas the year my younger daughter was seven, I got her an iguana,
but it died two days later, while her friend Zoe from across the street
had been left to look after him, as we were going upstate for the week.

It seems, for the whole time, although clearly it made no difference,
Zoe came everyday with her Mom, to change the food and water,
because she felt it was her duty, and perhaps with a shred of hope.
                (Later Zoe's mom had said, that yes, it had been a little odd,
                          coming each day, to feed a dead iguana.)

Last week, I spent several hours each day at the hospital visiting my Mother.
By that point her breathing had seemed to become at best dutiful;
mechanical like a beached Sea Robin in a morning shore wash.

Now and then as I sat alone with her, waiting,
I'd reach out to touch her arm;
and once or twice I told her I loved her, just in case it might still matter.

From time to time, I'd rearrange the few spare things on her bedside table—
the pictures I'd brought of the kids when they were little;
the flowers, the plastic pitcher; the cup, and the rolls of adhesive tape—

and sometimes I'd watch her just be there;
and randomly, her deep sunk eyes would half open,
drift slowly; and pass like wandering ghosts.

TOMATOES: A PARABLE

The man worried often about what people thought, for fear of never being loved.
    He would judge his own worth, and the things he cared for harshly;
        it was safer rather than to appear foolish,
        or to make some specious claim.

One day, while standing in his garden, a friend asked,
    "Oh," a little awkwardly, "you have ripe tomatoes already."
        "May I try one", she asked,
        "mine are all still green?"

"Go ahead", he replied, wanting to be polite, "They're OK I guess;
    nothing special.", careful not to overstate;
        as a child he had learned,
        one must be careful always.

"What do you mean," the woman asked, by then having tasted one,
    "they are good, sweet and delicious; what on earth do you expect?"
        The man was not sure, but something more.
        To him they had seemed just not quite right.

## THE GOOD NEWS IS


For weeks before, they had talked each night late
on telephones; alone, naked in their darkened rooms
on beds with rumpled cotton sheets,
                      once their children had gone off to sleep.


They had met, now and then, in some quiet restaurant, where
over candles, and a bottle of wine, they had held hands and slowly stroked
the softness of the other's forearm across a white tablecloth,
                      and looked deeply into one another's eyes.


Foolishly once again he had built unsteady fantasies; a place of sunsets,
and the scents of summer; a shared garden, and flesh to flesh—
late at night, and early mornings— in an upstairs room with fluttering curtains,
                      where nothing would ever have to be explained.


The good news is this time he had seen it coming; she had been clear about it all
from the start, she'd said, this time she wanted to find someone with money;
and he had hoped to somehow change her mind. It came hard the evening she called
                      to say she had snow found someone, and was moving on.


The day that followed he spent alone looking for hope in shallow streams of grief;
turning the endless ragged stones. The night had been long; and lost in wanderings;
a sleepless labyrinth, where his rage filled cries he laid half silent;
                      gnawed into his ravaged feather pillow.
                                  He longed to talk to her; to hold her.


In the late afternoon, of the autumn now already two weeks begun,
he walks the stone cobbled paths through a city park, in those final shafts of the warm
October sun waning; wanting—if for only this at the very least—
                      that the Indian Summer might somehow go on and on.

Later, as twilight falls, he sits alone at home remembering the dream
and those pieces he had pretended to ignore, back still when he had so hoped.
And there, as daylight ebbs, and the darkness again surrounds him; silently he aches,
and the dust motes once more slowly gather.

## JOURNAL ENTRY: SWEEPING THE PORCH IN EARLY APRIL

It has been busy here since very early,
with the in and out of an almost warming sun
        teasing now among the pre-budding of the apple trees.

Today I have been trying to clear the detritus
of the winter's littering, and regret
        I have to leave back to the city shortly;

a day that has been so rife with the struggles of Spring;
phoebes singing, in the mid-afternoon, between,
        the blizzarding, of insistent snow showers.

## CLOWNS AND GORILLAS

As a child, questions troubled the boy; people were not to be trusted
and so he found answers inside. The world had been made to fool him;
   he had known this for some time. The world was facades; actors changed costumes;
he made no mention of this to anyone;
                      it was safest, not to let them know all he had discovered.


Clowns frightened the boy; clowns were people like Chinese or gypsies,
but not exactly; mutations, a related species, like zebra to horses;
   a cabal, a skewed off tribal caste forced to live apart.
He worried what clowns might do,
                  if they found him watching.


It was wrong to stare; he knew, he had been so told many times.
Still often, in spite of this, he would watch: the nuns; the elderly in wheelchairs;
   men in service uniforms on crutches, or with missing limbs,
their sleeve or pant leg pinned up in half. Clowns he knew were sad too,
                he wondered where they lived.


The boy learned many things from the nature films and animated movies
his grandmother would take him to now and then after a lunch at Schrafft's.
   Sitting silently in flannel pants those afternoons in darkened theatres
fingering the velvet seats, the boy watched and looked for answers,
                wishing so his feet could only reach the floor.


On Saturdays, to allow his mother to sleep, the boy's father—
who wore suits even on weekends— would take the child in a sailor hat
   on morning trips. Frequently they might visit the city zoo,
and often they would stay for lunch.
                After lunch they would stop to visit the gorilla.

On the way, the father, would buy the boy a balloon and tie the string
to a button. Once the balloon had flown away; the boy had watched as it rose
 above the trees, fearful it would burst on the tip of a  far off building spire.
The gorilla upset the boy; it's dark eyes raised questions of deception;
                    how things truly are, versus how they may appear.


   To the boy it seemed the gorilla was a man forced inside a costume,
a creature-man perhaps, who they covered in blackened motor grease,
from a garage, like one he had seen with a naked lady near home.
Why was man inside being punished, the boy wondered;
                    what very bad thing he must have done?


   And though frightened, the boy felt sad for the creature, and wished he could help.
Silently from the barkless branch in the tiled cage, the  angry eyes watched.
  Small birds came; fearlessly they'd peck the discarded half oranges strewn
across the stained concrete floor. The father stood behind the boy,
                    and as always, sadly, offered no explanation.


   In the afternoon before they would leave for home, the boy in his sailor hat
would hold tight for a while, to the cool of the paint-chipped iron rail, and think:
   about the sea lions—they were the ones he wanted to be,
they always had so much fun— and how when Rosie died—the hippopotamus—
                    they had had to use a crane.

IN MY DREAM THIS MORNING

In my dream this morning
you and I were together
again in that same old house somewhere with its musty smell,
as it happens always, sometimes still.


And in that somewhere, it seemed you had changed
the light-bulbs upstairs, in the little boudoir
lamps nested on the veined marble dresser top
to ones of a more pinkish sort of hue, and so it seemed to signal:

>   you were back again;
>   and all that had passed had been now since forgotten.

ONE AFTERNOON WHILE VISITING
IN A SMALL PAINTED ROOM FILLED WITH FADED LIGHT


When the boy was still quite young—four or maybe five—he sat with the children of the house on a small woolen rug while his parents were entertained down the hall in a larger room with bookshelves, that overlooked a park. Leaves of the plane trees had only just begun to turn, and late September sun shafted the parquet floor through the open windows, and across the potted wax-begonia. The boy, as his parents saw such code as requisite, had been dressed for the occasion in grey flannel pants.

He had met the children before; the son, more than a year older than he, and the girl, who though a full year younger, was unusually mature—as women, even then, so frequently seemed could be— possessed deep truths, and a great knowledge in the secrets of the world; the boy, eager to learn, sat with rapt attention. Lacking other sport that afternoon, his hosts amused themselves teasing the boy, using their guest for little more than a dog might a stuffed toy. And so it all began that Indian Summer long ago.

Grinning, the older brother sat silently by, as his sister—already well schooled in the ways of engaging older men—looked their guest in the eye wordlessly. Enticing, intimating and suggesting with her intimacy, that there was crucial treasure, that she, her brother—perhaps a cadre of important people in the world—already held; and that now, miraculously he, the boy, had perhaps been selected by the great gatekeepers to be privy, and no longer but a mere outsider: and so it was; and so it was.

"Do you know what..??", the little girl asked half whispering; dramatically glancing first toward the door as if just-in-case. Whatever it was, the boy of course did not. And so—albeit more than somewhat trepidant as to his strength for handling such potential; as after all, he was still only just small — it was beyond trustingly that the boy with joyous gratitude looked back into the girls dark brown eyes, and without hesitation, heart in throat, breathlessly answered her; "What..??" The little girl was thrilled.

Giddy—hardly able to contain her triumphant joy as long as a full suspenseful pause—gleefully she responded, "That's what..", glanced to the older brother; the two laughed knowingly, and then fell silent. The boy felt lost. Left out betrayed and confused, he wondering what he perhaps once more had missed; anxious, he wordlessly waited for whatever might come next. In the corner of the darkening room, a cast iron radiator sat silent too. The boy in the grey flannel pants tried to suppose.

Was there a secret language or an unknown other something; so much in the world it seemed he was just not in on, and wished there might somehow be a second chance. Moments later, once more, the girl looked him in the eye seducing; "Do you know what..??". "What..??", he said—still heart-hopeful/unquestioningly trusting; knowing this time would be different, that this time she would say—and again she answered, "That's what..!!", the sibling laughed, and the cruel game went on and on for some time.

The girl and her brother, like beak-nosed jackals, circled their prey dangling hope, and the boy, so wanted, thanklessly would always reach; reckoning still each time it would be different, that the dues had been paid, and the promise land lay over the very next ridge—though in fact it never really is; nor in time do all good things somehow always come. In the end, later when darkness had fully descended, the little boy in the flannel pants was at last finally taken home.

QUALIFIERS


One night my freshman year in Philadelphia, when I was still a virgin,
this girl Liza invited me over, and got me really drunk;
she had said she had tequila, and that for sure it would get rid of my cold.

Liza was very pretty; she most always wore these gold hoop earrings,
had short, hennaed hair, and small upturned breasts
I had a hard time keeping my eyes off of.

My guess is I probably could have slept with her that night;
she had candles lit and music playing—Ravi Shankar, I think;
or maybe it was Monk or Bach, that part I really don't remember—

as we lay there on pillows, on a Batik spread she'd laid
carefully on that wooden floor; it was everything I had hoped for,
but after a while, somehow it all just was making me very afraid.

Around midnight, I wound up stumbling home along the empty streets,
wishing only that I would have stayed, though clear I had been just way too fearful:
of my lust, and of uncertainties; of change and of letting go, and moving finally on.

In truth though, I think mostly I was ashamed about being a virgin,
and appearing awkward;
though Liza, I'm pretty sure, gladly would have led me through.

That night in my bed alone, it felt safer —
under the corduroy cover I'd brought along with me from home—
familiar things, can make it seem that way, when fear locks you out from life.

Even now I look for certainty, before I commit to anything,
and then for a backup plan, to have just in case.
Certainties never seem to stay that way:
        right one minute wrong the next; now you see it, now you don't.

I think that's probably why I use so many qualifiers;
without them words just get too committed.
Commitment, I think should last forever; commitments are final like death.

## PAINTING THE HOUSE

Drew my younger daughter got her license three weeks back
and has been gone now mostly ever since;
Alex, the older one, is down working two jobs in the City;
she stays out late most nights; and is going back to college very soon.
I am going to miss her more this time I think;
and then next fall, Drew will be heading off as well.


The last few weeks I have been painting the house; it's been ten years
since the last time it got done; Drew has helped me out some now then.
Up here, time takes its toll on a hundred year old farmhouse; pitting
cedar clapboard, and the rotting aging trim, that now I scrape and paint again—
as others have as well—balancing on high extension ladders;
trying to hold on, as the summer cirrus clouds go ebbing past.


There were mountains of billowed clouds against the bright blue summer sky
this morning—blue like the underside of farmhouse porches—
now in this late August, after so many days of grey, threatened rain.
This summer is the wettest most can remember,
and the intermittent storms just further soak the over-sodden soil;
I've needed a fire most mornings, but my garden is doing pretty well.


Earlier today I found four bats hanging behind the louvered shutters
I was taking down to scrape. Bats hang upside-down they say,
because their legs are too weak to support them; nature often has peculiar ways.
I felt bad disturbing them from their shadowed home, that had come to feel was safe,
and theirs, secreted away; up here I find each creature seems more a fellow traveler,
and not really an adversary.


As I paint—rather than swatting at them—I ask the spiders, and wasps
(and what have you) to please move on; and in a while, I find that generally they will.
In time the bats flew off, though one kept on returning. Diving and swooping past,
it seemed so angry and afraid; not knowing where else to go, and desperately wanting
to return, to a place that just wasn't there anymore.
At nearly sixty now, it is unlikely I will ever do this job again.

Yesterday morning I wept out loud several times while reading
that Donald Hall book, "String to Short To Be Saved",
it all seemed way too close, I guess. It is all about how time moves on;
kids grow up, things change; and all our monuments to continuity
eventually fall to irrelevance—no matter how well they were conceived;
no matter how hard we work to make them last.


But now, by the pond, the surface is all but still, and as the sun lowers
past the ridge board of the barn—beyond
the cattails, and the ancient maples;
the goldenrod, and asters just coming into bloom—I watch
a darning needle pass, hovering for an instant, and then it is gone;
and hope, whomever it is that paints here next, thinks I did an OK job.


There is a hatch of a mayfly by the dock, swarming in its ritual dance;
ecstatic as troupe of dervishes, and with meaning we can only guess at.
And now a baby duck just landed by the far side, lost
and calling out; it moves oddly through the water as it swims—
hurt perhaps and wanting to be saved—
wanting to be cared for and protected in this uncertain world.


The fall before last, I put in raised beds in my vegetable garden.
I am proud of them; it seems they have worked out really well.
Most days I'll go out there to check on how things are coming along;
weed, and thin what's gotten overcrowded, and stake what seems to needs support.
This summer almost everything has flourished, except the okra;
this far north, I suppose okra is an awful lot to ask.


Gardening can teach a lot about our limits, and how to face the truths the way they are.
In the end, probably, it is a lot of what Candide has in mind, when he says to Pangloss,
"..but we must all go work in our garden."; important stuff we all need to try to learn.
Up here our growing season is short, and so I plant a lot, and harvest what I can;
tending a garden can at least let you try to believe
you have control over how things move along.

## WRITING IN WATER

It had been just the first time that they had met,
and she had told him, among the many things,
about the calligraphy masters she had seen in China;

the way they stand in a Beijing park, with one hand on a hip,
as they glide their long-handled brushes—as if tiny pointed mops—
across the paving stones, in strokes that dance in sensuous staccatos.

She told of how they draw the characters, day after day with incalculable intricacy;
their brushes dipped in only water, as it is always only just for practice,
and all but that which is learned, forever will quickly disappear.

The implication of her story had now stayed with him for days.
That which remains is only the lesson to be had from the moment;
whatever else there is beyond that, has no real worth,
      still we grasp so desperately to hold onto something more.

That night, as they had sat and talked for hours effortlessly
over two glasses of wine, their arms touched from time to time—
a little awkward yet, but more purposeful than what comes just by simply chance—
      he had wanted so much for it all to last.

Walking her home across the lamp-lit park, they had lingered,
and talked some more, on that oddly warm star-risen October evening,
as the first sliver of a waxing moon hung suspended overhead.

In time they had gently kissed goodnight;
and with arms lightly wrapped around one another,
she, on a second breath, had pressed to him, a little longer than really expected.

Varied wanderers passed—some in couples arm in arm;
some alone, or with dogs out for the last time until morning—
their shoes resounding, and then lost to distance (absorbed in the hollow darkness)
      as he continued alone along the long shadowed paths.

## TO MY MOTHER

In the end, you looked so silly lying there;
your hands folded across your chest
    with those spindly half-dead mums,
    that some attendant must have laid on you, taken from the trash—
    wilted, and browned at the edges;
    only there to play the role—
    at death, folded hands and flowers, I guess is how it's supposed to be.

I just stood and watched you lying there;
your eyes were open,
    and it all was very out of keeping—
    appearing more as a wax double of you,
    but certainly not real thing—
    so gently quiet, so hollowed out already;
    as if mostly nothing much was left, of any real worth.

I thought about just a few hours back,
how still your breath had been unreasonably determined:
    by then it seemed so pointless;
    and truly I couldn't understand why.
    Just grit I suppose—you were never one to just take things as they come—
    and in the end, as my friend Eddie said,
    letting go, must be very hard.

There in that darkened room—
just me alone with you, and the single bedside lamp—
    I made myself touch your face
    in case there was some conscious part of you still lingering.
    It was hard to do, but it seemed just somehow right;
    and that it might figure in how I'd be judged,
    at some point down the line.

There was so much I wish had been different between us—
but it wasn't—and now of course it seems that, that is that.
    Probably I should have brought along some decent flowers;

                                    yes I guess, maybe, I suppose.

REFLECTION, AUGUST 1st 2008: ON NASA'S ANNOUNCEMENT:
OF WATER ON MARS AND THEREFORE POSSIBILITY OF LIFE


Who is there to say that rocks do not in fact have lives,
or those endless unknown quantities,
                      beyond our wildest dreams;

starless dimensions, among the wandering unrelated galaxies, expanding;

                      into futures, and into pasts.

Septillions of yet unknown divisions
within each atom nuclei of say, the tiniest known of bacterium—
are there not incalculable worlds that seethe with prosaics and complex existence;

and knowledge and physics
                      eclipsing all we will ever know;

making us, seem something, only close to quaint.


                      And all those wounded lives like ours,

        with their lonely longings, loves and secret fears;

are they not too linked to nothing, and everything—always to forever—

                      yes, but then who is there to say.

## IT WAS EIGHTEEN DEGREES HERE THIS MORNING

It was eighteen degrees here this morning,
and there now is a wind rippled skim of ice
that has settled on the pond below my house.

The skim will likely be gone by mid-afternoon;
though then again, maybe not.
It is hard to tell when winter will take its final hold.

Earlier, the sun shone orange on the tree line
to the upper fields beyond
the long fallow meadow deep-dusted now with snow.

Today, the anxious hunters—decked out in gear of camouflage and orange blaze—
will pace on wooden porches, and wait expectantly;
readying for the Monday dawn.

They will all go off to the woods bravely that first day of rifle season—
to kill their deer, or try— they with larders already filled,
and their wives safely back at home.

I instead, in the quiet cold, will do my final chores—
and resign to the inevitable end—just before the hard frost
sets and takes charge of the last vestiges of all what still remains.

I will bring in the garden hose, and gather kindling,
in preparation—
facing death, in a different sort of way, I guess—

while the last dried wildflowers along the road hold to yesterday's
errant snow, masquerading—for all the world—
as cotton stalks, in the cold November wind

## GLASSES

For me the greatest problem with wearing glasses has never been just one of vanity,
in fact (right or wrong) I've always thought I looked pretty OK when I've had them on;
so yes, while there is that major nuisance of how they are forever dirty—
and steam over in winter, whenever you come in from outside—

for me, the major downside is I have come to realize;
being nearsighted, I have to take them off to read.
Therefore, if I am on the subway say, or a park bench reading—
with a sandwich, or a cup of take-out tea in spring—

when a woman passes who catches my eye
(which even at this age, I am afraid to say, still all too many do)
freshly piqued interest, forces me foolishly
to put the glasses back on in hope of finer detail;

first feigning a random glance towards some sliver of drama
at the other end of the rumbling car, in hope
my furtive prurience is not so immediately conspicuous.
A moment perhaps, toward the sneezing child, or the snoring mariachi,

or the frayed Abruzzese gentleman, who wanders along
the park's long winding paths, lined with gum-stained hexagonal stone.
He feeds the pigeons as he travels; tossing the stale breadcrumbs purposefully
from his worn brown-paper bag, and a wooden cane hooked to his forearm.

In spite of everything, I never learn to leave well enough alone.
Almost always with sharpened vision, I wind up sadly
disappointed by that which had been only moments prior,
likely it seemed, the final answer to my prayers.

Wearing glasses endlessly underscores
how much of life can be more satisfying
when left just a blurry gist we tailor,
to fit in more appealing ways within romantic longings.

ALGEBRA

Once when I told a woman things weren't really working out,
she asked,
        "Would it have been different if I had let you sleep with me?"

The truth was I didn't think so, but I lied,
I said, I didn't know,
        which, was also true too, I guess.

But the real truth mainly was,
we had arrived at a point in the dance, when the steps get way too hard;
        in any case, you can't resolve things backwards,
              work out the final moves and expect the rest
                      somehow to just fall into place.

It seems this stuff is all like algebra, where as I remember,
        the problem's answer is already known
              and yet you still have to find the way:

                you must work through all the pieces, following ordered protocols;
                you can not just jump ahead, you just go one step at a time.


                Algebra is like stroking velvet against the grain;
                there are ways things go, and ways they don't.

# AT JOE THE BARBER'S

On Saturdays sometimes now and then when I was still quite small, my father —who dressed in suits on weekends even—took me uptown for a haircut, to Joe the barber's, the place he always went. The shop was one flight up on the mezzanine level of the Commodore Hotel, next to Grand Central Station; it was huge like a mirrored ballroom, that even then, in the early fifties, seemed left from a time long since passed. There were, best I remember, dozens of barber's chairs with deep leather upholstery, and tooled hardware fittings of nickel-plated brass, that sat poised before their lavish cabinetry. Altars crafted in stippled stone and mahogany; shelves lined in pomades and unguents, and drawers that housed mysterious tools of the trade. In flannel pants— awkwardly; clench-fisted—I would enter the daunting grown-up world of tailored gentlemen, and there across the room, thick in the erotic in the scents of witch-hazel and steam, would be Joe, my father's barber at his spot; a Hungarian I believe. His meticulous hair was always parted just so, and he would greet us, doting like a Pullman porter; his shoulder-buttoned tunic embroidered, 'The Terminal Barber Shop', and below that, his name in red hued thread, stitched in cursive script; a red that I in time would learn to know as Madder Lake Deep.

Carefully I would climb up onto a child seat that Joe placed straddled across the arms of his tall leather chair, and my father would sit in the one next to me and watch by way of beveled mirror on the wall. As he sat, he would have his nails pared and lacquered by a blond manicurist, in her starched crisp-white uniform and seamed nylon stockings—washed each night with a bar of Ivory in her fourth floor walk-up bathroom sink in Queens, and hung on the shower curtain rod to dry; stockings that each day with more than full understanding, she would cross, and re-cross suggestively. His fingertips she would first soak in a little silver bowl a ruffled paper liner, changed for each client, no doubt for hygiene's sake, and I would watch as she held to his hands with such convincing purpose, plying her enterprise—wishing one day for all this too—filing and buffing with curious instruments she carried station-to-station in a box-like tray, she then rested carefully balanced on one knee, with an ease only acquired after long practice of the skill. And from time-to-time —above the working clatter, and banter of shallow conversation in that man-filled room—a muffled clang of the polished towel steamer being opened or closed, that stood apart with its daunting gas-flame jets secreted inside; a hard swallowed sound, punctuating the room's Saturday quotidian din.

## TWO DAYS LATER:
## AFTER THE FIGHT WITH THE RABBID RACCOON

My cat Louise may never have been all that smart, but for sure she was a love.
It was so hard that day I had to have her put down; it had been no way her fault,
and she seemed still pretty much OK.

Outside the curtained waiting room window, birds sang,
their chuntering songs, and the sun shone brightly;
inside its pine paneled walls, it was just me and Louise,
with those magazines, and molded chairs on the tiled linoleum floor;
me and Louise alone amid the long lingering scents of alcohol and cedar,
and the hollow of a deep-felt silence we shared:
and the ticking of the unseen wall-clock, somewhere in another room.

That end of August afternoon,
Louise looked to me so trustfully as I held her
there on the stainless steel examining table,
and Dr. Nydam prepared his syringes for what now had to be done.
Over and over, I had to lie to her eye-to-eye; I had to tell her everything would be okay.

Dear Louise; trusting so deeply, even as the injections began to take their hold;
she—
like all of us somehow I guess; in spite of everything—
wanting so much to still believe.

BRENDA

UPSTATE SOLDIER KILLED IN IRAQ, the headline read, or something like it;
Metro section February 20th, 2005, and how it was his second tour there in Iraq.

The columnist said that she had seen it somehow fitting that this Army sergeant,
Christopher M. Pusateri, who had looked forward to a career in the military,

was proud to be serving his country, that his life had ended days before in gunfire,
and that he had been born on the fourth of July.

We are told his wife Christine (age 20), learned of her husband's dying
that same evening when two uniformed officers had come to their Fort Bragg home.

Christine, it said, had known what had happened the moment she saw the men
approaching, but confused on how she could react.

Christopher and Christine Pustieri (*Chris and Chris*); they had been
high school sweethearts, married on Valentine's Day two years prior.

The sergeant's mother, Brenda West (39, Corning, NY), said how everyone had been
anxiously awaiting her son returning home.

She recalled her son as sensitive, someone who cared about looking after others
and, always hoped everybody might be proud of him.

She mentions too how when Pusateri was a boy, that he had enjoyed Dungeons and
Dragons, and that she had been upset when he signed his induction papers.

It was just another story, hid deep in a mid-week Metro Section; a brief blurb
about yet another now dead soldier, and a few other upstate people I never knew.

But Brenda, I thought, just thirty-nine, not much more than a child herself;
probably pretty, and too young for me to date.

AFTER

Although her family all had insisted that it would never matter,
And how they wanted him to stay close always,
Even then, after she had left him for someone else;

And though the younger sister—ten years younger,
Aware each marriage has difficulties of there own—
Said, she knew there was more than one side to the story;
                                    and yes of course there was, and always is;

And her Mother, with whom he had so sweetly bonded—
Those steamed-up window, holiday kitchen afternoons—
and who had clearly loved him, still in those first few months after;

And despite the heart-to-heart long-distance conversations
On the phone with the older sister in her central Colorado home,
Whose dark brown eyes he felt all welled with understanding;

And the brother too in Pennsylvania,
Who said each time they spoke how he hoped
That this, nor anything, would come to interfere between them;

Still a few years later, they all it seemed had abandoned him,
The family— who on all those Christmas hoarfrost mornings—
Had so felt also his, and by then for more than twenty years.

# THOUGHTS ON THE FURTHER WISDOM OF POSTPONING JOY, AND HOW AT 63 IT MIGHT NOW BE TIME TO CASH IN MORE

At breakfast today P, I opened that raspberry jam, Marilynn had given me a year ago;
I particularly love her raspberry, and I had been saving it;
but for what I'm not exactly sure, maybe it's been just to know that it was there.

We exchange canning, me and Marilynn;
there is a kind of sweet bravado in the process.
And I at least reuse the empty Ball jars; for me it is part of how it's all supposed to go.

A while back I called my high school friend Nancy,
it was a Sunday, and I asked what she was up to;
she and I have breakfast, three or four times a year.

Nancy said she had just taken the set of buttons
from a worn out pair of pajamas— she said—
to maybe use, at some point down the line.

*Waste not, want not / idle hands are the devil's workshop;*
*a penny saved, a penny earned / a stitch in time save nine.*

Part of all this of course is thrift;
with thrift and work come some certain comforts: a hope of karmic wealth accruing;
tickets punched; points to cash, at a needy time.

Hedging bets, I tend to save all sorts of random things;
recycling has an underpiece of immortality that seems to tag along.
I guess we all seek some sense of things going on for always:
                      you know like love, and art and kids; so on and what have you.

Some days a conflict goes on inside me; holding on, versus simply starting new.
Once I remember was walking home and hearing fire trucks;
and had hoped it was my house burning, and that everything would be lost.

To me, it always felt like Grandma Moses, in the end had her life work out really well;
and how like with dessert, it was
that the sweetest part came, after all the rest had passed.

And so P, last week, driving around in Italy with you,
it seemed my cards had now come out pretty OK as well.
You were so close, and all that beauty;

        and as we drove, now and then, your hand would slip beneath my thigh.

ABANDONED GARDENS

There is this recurrent dream I have sometimes;
in it I'm at home somewhere (though no place I've ever really lived)
and notice flower beds out back, which in the past I had tended to dutifully,
                      but realize now I hadn't looked after in quite some time.

The part I think that makes this dream interesting,
is the realization gets me guilt-filled, and afraid, of how the world will judge me,
I assume because the world will now see the truth about me,
                      i.e. the way things in fact really are.

*Dreams, they say all have to do with something,*
        *and each facet manifests some aspect of the self.*

In the dream it seems that if I can clean up the garden quickly—
rake out the withered stalks and the years of windblown leaves—
put in a few flats of annuals (to make things look right again)
                    then no one maybe will really have to know;

                      and once more will have fooled them,
                      and be safe again, at least for a little while.

RESONANCE ON THE FIRST DAY OF SPRING: 2006

On the weather report, they said today on the first day of spring,
"Snow is falling again in the Midwest", they said,
"More than a foot, already in Nebraska", a place I only remember

as a two-lane macadam, through an endless flatland strewn in dead jackrabbits,
driving west once to Colorado, on a moonless night in June of 1965;
but that was then, and long ago.

Here upstate now, it's maple sugar time; cold nights, follow warming days.
This morning earlier, I saw blades of daffodils starting
up through the last of winter; skewering the blanketing of leaves from autumns past,

and a fresh snow dusting from the night before.
Later, I will drive my younger daughter back to school,
and then sadly, I won't see her again, at least until mid-May.

This past week, I watched the Jim Jarmusch movie, "Broken Flowers",
upstairs on my bed in the city; alone with pillows propped against the wall.
I must say I thought it was pretty something, and in truth, it also kind of made me cry.

Near the end, this guy Don Johnston (fifty, maybe) played by Bill Murray,
says this Buddha sort of thing; he has been off some time on a road trip
in search of clues to a possible son he had never known he had.

One-by-one, he shows up unannounced at the homes of the four important women
in his life twenty years back. He brings to each them a large bouquet of flowers;
all are changed, and with none could there likely be redemption.

Tensions ramps up quite a bit when the daughter of one of the women
greets Johnson at the door, in only an ultra-short robe and platform mules;
the mother is not yet home, and the girl is barely younger than her mother
                    had been twenty years ago.

We are made uneasy when the girl seats Murray on the living room recliner,
then disappears to answer a ringing phone offstage. A bit later she returns stark naked;
half teasing—as she chats on her cordless receiver—but mostly oblivious,
                    because he is far too old to really matter anymore.

Anyway, there is this scene toward the end of the movie,
by then having spoken with all four women,
he, though what seems some providence of chance, meets up with this drifter kid.

In the scene, the man has gone into a café and bought the boy a sandwich;
two bottles of water, and a coffee to go, in a brown paper bag. The sandwich is
vegetables, mushroom and cheese; we have some assumption the boy may be his son.

As they sit outside while the boy is eating, he asks the man
what advise he might have to give him for the road:

> *The past is gone,"* the man tells him, *"I know that…*
>
> *The future, whatever it is going to be, isn't here yet.*
> *So, this is all there is, the present.",*
> and that was all.

The man just so helplessly wanting to provide something meaningful
—as I believe we all hope to—
trying somehow ultimately to matter.

Last week, for three days I watched a pigeon
dying on a ledge across the street from my bedroom window.
I wasn't sure what, but I kept feeling

> I should have done something for him,
> and then one morning he was gone.

## SHE WASN'T THERE AGAIN THAT MORNING

She wasn't there again that morning when he woke
She said the night before she couldn't sleep
It had been too hot and loud she said
That she had moved downstairs to the couch
Stared first at the ceiling and then past
The ceiling and all the other floors
    Then through the roof where she had watched the stars for a while


It had been beautiful there she said, all the lights
It had been like camping by that stream upstate
In Arkville a few weeks back
But then she had heard him stir upstairs she said
It had brought her back and had felt so trapped
Again inside a metal box with no light at all
    Often then when she spoke her terrible sadness made him very afraid

FALL COLOR

In mid-October upstate here
—past first frost, and now the garden down—
it is the yellows mainly, that blanket everywhere.

Now the back country roads are all but obscured
beneath the yellow leaves abundance, and likewise lawns
last mown three weeks back, that lay

and wait, first to brown, and then too soon to be laden white with snow.
The world, quieter then, will go to colorless shades,
and only the hopeful greens of the spruce and hemlock will remain.

By mid-October, the trees—save the few still half verdant;
blazed with dappled shocks of scumbled orange,
and brilliant crimsoned hues, against a cloud filled sky —

are mostly turned and losing their ochre leaves already;
seemingly more and more each day. The leaves quavering,
and holding on as best they can in the lead grey north blowing winds.

Like autumn color, nature provides us wisdom:
a consolation prize for our loss of youth;
a brightening, before the dark fading of our end.

And in these last moments before the party sadly ends,
I look up and watch it all, as I put on the storm windows once again,
and carry the cordwood to hold me safely;  preparing
                                        for a long cold time to come.

## AFTER A SECOND DATE WITH A WOMAN WITH WHOM I KNEW THINGS WOULD LIKELY GO NOWHERE

Earlier we had been to see that Mike Nichols movie "Closer";
    a dark film of beautiful couples, who first fall in love,
deceive each other, then return to ask for truth.
    Like all of us thought, in truth all they really want is affirmation;
to hold tight to in hope
    to quell our darkest doubts.


We talk about it all at a bar with candles burning after,
    me and this woman, as if in some telling David Mamet moment—
each of us playing our hopeful, tattered parts—
    sitting side by side in the low-lit wine bar;
fingering our long stemmed glasses of Shiraz,
    and with our arms almost touching from time to time.


Halfway through the first glass she says to me—
    this almost too lean woman, ten years younger, maybe more—
*"Women"*, she says—
    and so I assumed she was speaking from self-knowledge;
as she ran her long tapered fingers once through that auburn hair,
    and then again, and once more for authority, trying to win her point—


*"all are liars."*, and then asks, how it was that I didn't I know it;
    that her seventeen year old son certainly did.
*"They use every tool at their disposal"*,
    she says, half joking but not really, and disdains
that I am a hopeless romantic that if by now I didn't realize this too—
    which half pridefully, half in shame—I freely admit to be true.


Our candle flickered some
    as the barman poured us each another glass
while the evening dream scenario I had devised receded
    further into the dark abyss where others, over time, had and come and gone.
Soon, I walked her to the corner and we each departed on our way;
    home alone, our glasses emptied, and both seeming tired of the play.

"*People,*" Mamet says—speaking of truth, and manipulation—
    as I read later on that evening, "*may
or may not say what they mean
    ...but they always say something designed
to get what they want.*" It was I thought, in context, pretty worth noting,
    and goes, I guess, really without saying.

BEYOND MIDDLE AGE

I'm afraid the hard reality is—
    despite a predilection to the contrary,
        and in spite of all what one might hope to think—

once a man has reached a certain age,
    the only women who might seriously be going out with them,
        will be just a bunch of old ladies; and that is pretty much no matter what.

## I SEE YOU STILL

       I see you still: in those cotton summer dresses,
and your parted, wavy chestnut hair,
and the way you would sit alone on the courtyard grass,
    reading with those particular pretty sandals there beside you;
    you were so different, but of course I knew so very little about you.

       Do you remember that you scratched my back from the bottom up
that one evening before you left, as we sat those sultry hours
on the wooden floor, in that mousy apartment you had on Pine Street;
    the rest I know was mostly kind of just my dreamings,
    and in truth there was really nothing more.

       I longed for you so much that summer after you had left.
Poland, then Paris; I wrote to you probably too often.
You would write back some, but then it was less and less.
    Eight-to-ten weeks became a year, and then a little more,
    and by the end I'd been all but certain I'd never see you again.

       Do you remember that carton I sent to you in Paris
with all the customs declarations; treasures I had bought for you in Chinatown—
cans of roots, and oils and sauces—with labels impossible to read,
    and had hoped it would make you think lovingly of me.
    Something leaked you said, and that was about all.

       It was in June, a year later, that you called. You had just returned, you said
I was so surprised and so glad to hear your voice. Six-thirty, you said,
I should come to your parents house the following night for dinner;
    and though I'd started seeing someone else,
    I was still so very lost in you.

     I walked there that following evening, looking forward so to seeing you,
as the sun across the river began to lower, and a glow shown over the red brick houses
along your Chelsea street. That evening though, I felt you were locked away
    in a deep and quiet sadness, and my awkward feelings left me too afraid to call.
For years we passed on streets but never spoke; perhaps I read you wrong.


     But still on that sweet June night, when we barely, barely touched;
sorrowfully I left on the road I would regret for so many years to come.
You stood, backlit in that brownstone kitchen
    and made salad dressing, with a raw egg in a jar;
      another something that I held to, and had never seen before.

## DEADHEADING THE COSMOS

A while earlier when I came back in to my studio
trying to get down to work after tending to the garden,
checking on the tomatoes, deadheading the cosmos,
and all the things that it seems I need to do every day,

I thought a bit about the dinner I'd be making later for ten,
half of whom had never been over before. For them I'd mowed the lawn,
and damp-rag cleaned the house with soap and ammonia, worried
what they all might think, and wanting everything to seem just so.

I find myself thinking about Morandi—his entire life painting those bottles,
and finding his life's true meaning among the shapes that grew in-between.
Day after day alone in his Bologna bedroom, I wondered if it ever troubled ever him,
or if he worried what people would think; painting that silent world over and over,
                           and in the end signing his name in a large cursive hand.

I will probably think about him too as I start preparing dinner; to damp my doubt
for the meal I had planned out days before, in hope to please and impress.
*I'm doing mussels, chicken, pasta, and what have you, just variations on stuff I've done a million*
*times; it seems safest with a new crowd, to sing the songs you know the best.*

After, when the dishes all are done, and glasses sit to dry, I will climb
the stairs to my second story room, to turn out the lights and sleep.
There I will think about the evening, and the day;
ends and beginnings, and roads not taken;

and then in time about women; one I wish might be here with me
tonight, while the crickets whisper to the moon, now two nights past full.
It lays a satin ribbon across my mirrored dresser; and Taurus sits low to the horizon,
with the crab Nebula riding proudly between his horns.

EPIPHANY: WITH A SHELL-CUT TOE

Lonesomely as I walk
        barefoot through the wave break
        in the early purple dawn

salt froth softly furrows stinging
        the small cut between my toes
        and shore breezes gently sway

treetop fingers of the tall coco palms
        how like mine their lonely longing
        groping for more even here in paradise

ON HAVING RETURNED TO THE CITY LAST NIGHT
WITH 16-24 INCHES OF SNOW FORECAST UPSTATE
STILL DRAWN TO THE ONE WHO IS UNAVAILABLE

I had just called to talk to you,
who I know (in spite of my wishing it were otherwise)
wants to keep things, 'just as friends',

and now seek some small solace in the residue of scent
of wood-fire on a worn plaid flannel shirt,
while outside rain torrents, and the cobbled gutters stream.

I think of that other woman; who had e-mailed to me earlier,
she was in western Massachusetts, she'd said; for the weekend;
snowed in with friends she'd know since college days.

Not really wanting to, I wonder
if now at least I should maybe call.
It's Sunday; it's so very quiet here.

## JUST A NOTE FROM TODAY

Up here now at six o'clock the sun sifts through
        the trees intermittently, this time of year,
        as they begin their turn, and speak so sadly
        about the coming of the summer's end.

When I arrived at the house, now only hours back,
        I saw how during the week, the giant cosmos had fallen;
        the thick stem snapped, but some threads inside remain,
        and so it seems to be carrying on.

The impatiens are lasting too, in spite of weather,
        and the black-eyed Susan;
        the cleome have grown the size of a small child's head,
        and the sunflowers, still so much larger.

This afternoon, I got two coats of paint, on those new shutters
        I made for the woodshed, last week in the city,
        and picked a basket of tomatoes in the garden,
        the last twigs of broccoli, and the final yellow squash.

The mowing, and my other chores, will have to wait until tomorrow,
        since soon the sun will set, and then I will finally go inside:
        but these are the things I do here, mostly;
        these are the things I love.

And now as the sun descends, triangulating light across the weathered reds—
        of the milk-house, brightly below my kitchen window;
        and shafts among the willow, and long edged blades of meadow grass,
        glistening the cupped fingers of the first fallen leaves on the uncut lawn,
                        and soon the dew begins—

it's you, dear dreamed of someone, it's you right now I am thinking of,
        as the last of the daylight fades and the early stars begin;
        it's you, just you, I wish were here right now,
        to hold, and to share it all with me.

AN AUTUMN REQUIEM

*The land would all be brindled then;*
*that was the consolation of Autumn, the trade;*
*and like wisdom, comes also,*
*only as lives begin to fade.*

Once more, that night Ayree fell to bed, exhausted; the day had gone with so little getting done. Summer was hard that way, days were long, but they passed so quickly. And soon summer—that now seemed still had just only begun—would again be over, and all the hopes for next year, from last, would fade again, and once more have to wait.

And he thought about seasons and endings, about death and replenishing, and how one morning a month from now, he'd see the first red edged leaves on a sugar maple somewhere, foretelling the end. Autumn always had made him sad; everything died, and only the promise of what again went unfulfilled remained. And then he turned and went to sleep.

## JOURNAL ENTRY: AFTER A LIGHT SEPTEMBER RAIN

This morning early, after a light September rain,
when the meadow lay blanketed grey in mists
of fog and the last of the purple aster;

a shaft of light cut bright and hard across the sways
of stiffening goldenrod that slowly rust and brown
heralding the end of the virescent summer;

the light, its sharpened edge defining
how deep there is darkness,
and that it is always, all too soon to come.

Alan Herman is native New Yorker, who now splits his time between downtown Manhattan and a farmhouse upstate, where mostly he mows, cuts firewood, and gardens.

Feeding the writing is a background in visual art—both sculpture and painting— with work that has been exhibited widely, and represented in various private and corporate collections, museums, and other public institutions.

Alan Herman holds BFA and MFA degrees, has recieved an NEA Endowment, enjoys time with his daughters, cooking for friends, red wine, and warm conversation.

This is his second collection of poetry.